Anonymous

A Collection of Songs and Madrigals

By English composers of the close of the fifteenth century

Anonymous

A Collection of Songs and Madrigals
By English composers of the close of the fifteenth century

ISBN/EAN: 9783337264833

Printed in Europe, USA, Canada, Australia, Japan

Cover: Foto ©Thomas Meinert / pixelio.de

More available books at **www.hansebooks.com**

SONGS AND MADRIGALS

OF THE

FIFTEENTH CENTURY.

300 Copies printed, of which this is No. _210_

nobis, puni sue patroni que
ritulis distui. V̅ Salue lignum

in crlignu ferre mundi preciu

V̅ Couvte isti plebi xp̄i crua
uenerut. Oue. Cion a

pirri et filio et spū tui sine
V̅ Impletu dñr. V̅ Xp̄ius tecua
V̅ crux uue spea
queut hoc mcruacoig maiore
V̅ Celtina V̅ V̅ be de lignua
co ouiuq̄ erit mecio. Antiphon̄.

O crux uruectisicta que
foull fuisti cligna porta

re rigali celorum et coustantin

alle luia q̄ ouiugat̄

O crux gloriosa o

crux adoranda o lignum

preciosum et admilum ui

te lignum pir

quod ad isia tolus cu

uictus et mundus xp̄i sau

guine redumptus alle

luia. S. A. E.
V̅ Dore iu medio
elo l̄ V̅ qui ḡ
nobis filiacoui
suicib̄ de fui
nis. Inueni A lleluia sal ue

lenuq crux salue alle

A COLLECTION

OF

SONGS

AND

MADRIGALS

BY

ENGLISH COMPOSERS

OF THE CLOSE OF THE

FIFTEENTH CENTURY.

PREPARED FOR THE MEMBERS OF

THE PLAINSONG AND MEDIÆVAL MUSIC SOCIETY.

LONDON:

PUBLISHED BY BERNARD QUARITCH, 15, PICCADILLY, W.

1891.

PREFACE.

*T*HE Songs and Madrigals contained in this volume, and exemplifying the state of English Musical Art at the close of the fifteenth century, are taken from MSS. in the British Museum, which are well known to antiquarians but not to musicians in general. It is hoped that the specimens here given may create a wider interest than now exists in Mediæval English Music, and so justify the publication by degrees in extenso of all our early music still in existence. Some of the Madrigals were reproduced by Stafford Smith in the year 1779, but his translation of the old notation is often defective and unreliable. No. 7, by King Henry VIII., is given in the form in which it appears on fol. 53 of Add. MSS. 31922 as an instrumental piece; but on fol. 49 of the same MS. a shorter version is given with words as the Madrigal—"If love now reigned." The same MS. contains a version of the song "Ah! the sighs" as the middle part of a Madrigal, but with the melody somewhat modified to suit the counterpoint.

The words of the Madrigals have not been altered except in spelling and, in one instance, where a modification was necessary for a modern audience. They are not reproduced on the Plates of the ancient notation, as, unless this were done in absolute facsimile, no value would attach to the reproduction. The text is often very irregularly written in the original, but in the translation the syllables have been allocated as closely as possible to their proper notes. The words of the Songs have been more modernized, and verses omitted; they are therefore printed below in their original form. The accompaniments to the Songs have been written specially for this work by Dr. C. W. Pearce.

SONGS AND MADRIGALS OF THE FIFTEENTH CENTURY.

I.—THE MUSIC.

IN the Original Manuscript the songs are unbarred, and unaccompanied. The melodies are characterized generally by a natural and graceful musical expression of the words, whilst their diatonic simplicity will be particularly grateful to ears unaccustomed to anything but the chromatic gorgeousness of modern music. Three of the seven are distinctly pastoral; viz :—" Kitt hath lost her Kye," "In May," and "The little pretty nightingale." Their music might almost be described as the counterpart in sound of some of the well-known Arcadian scenes of Watteau. The remaining four are more or less of an amorous nature, and express the love sighs as faithfully as though the music had been written but yesterday. Several of the songs have such an extended vocal range that it is somewhat difficult to assign them to any particular kind of voice (*see* "In May"); hence it is not unlikely that these may have been written specially for some particular singer of the day, a circumstance which has tended to exercise a power over composers of all times; and from which influence musicians of the present time are not exempt. In one or two places, the leap of a fourth is successively taken twice in the same direction, thus forming the interval of a seventh with but one note between its two—a melodic progression which is regarded at the present day as being rather unvocal.

The long pneuma-like prolongation of the last syllable of each verse may be construed in two ways; either

(1) The concluding bars of melody might have been "vocalized" with the final vowel of the last word in each verse, or,

(2) The last line of words might have been repeated by being sung to the concluding bars of music left in the original with no words beneath them.

In this edition, a line of continuation indicates the first method, and, for the sake of those singers who prefer the second method, the last line of words has been printed in smaller type *above* the music.

The symphonies and accompaniments have been written especially for this Work, the style of harmonization being of course strictly diatonic.

It will be interesting to note that several of the songs, "Kitt hath lost her Kye," "In May," and "Alone I live," have a formal design which anticipates, in a great measure, the Aria form of Handel and his cotemporaries, *i.e.*, with a first and second part, followed by a *Da Capo al Segno:* the others are in the short Ballad form resembling that of a Hymn Tune.

The Madrigals will be found interesting to the student of Musical History, from the fact that they exhibit in a striking degree the every-day practice of 15th Century composers. These musicians were contrapuntists rather than harmonists, *i.e.*, they were in the habit of adding part to part, melody against melody, rather than accompanying one principal air or tune with a mere succession of chords. Although the very act of causing two or three independent parts or melodies to be sung together necessarily produced a succession of more or less complete chords, the harmonic total thus obtained was regarded as incidental or secondary, and subservient to the interest excited by the individual and simultaneous procession of several distinct melodies; each of which, if heard apart from its fellows, might be looked upon as almost a tune by itself.

Music written in such a manner may, at first sight, appear to afford the composer but little scope for either variety or expression. It must not, however, be supposed that the several parts or melodies were flung together with no regard for *ensemble* effects. The device of *Imitation* alone was quite enough to ensure not only variety, but also sympathy, cohesion, and unity amongst the parts. By its means, one part might rest for awhile, the others still going on; and the fresh entry of the part temporarily silenced, now being heightened in effect by the use of a figure of melody previously sung by one of the other voices, could not fail to be interesting to the listener as well as to the performer. Nor was this all to be gained by *Imitation.* The continual thinning and thickening of the music caused by one or more voices resting and re-entering was, in itself, a means of imparting a pleasant variety of light and shade to the composition; whilst the emphatic confirmation of the sentiment of the words, caused by their reiteration in successive imitative entries, was a means of obtaining a unanimity of expression not to be gained in any other way. The same words repeated by voice after voice will often produce a greater effect of unanimous expression of feeling, than if heard in one simultaneous utterance. Such an effect was afterwards to be carried to its highest development in the Vocal Fugues of later masters as Handel, J. S. Bach, Mozart, Mendelssohn, and others. The less artistic (because more easily obtainable), devices of *Sequence* and *Pedal-point,* also find exemplification in these pages. A *Sequence* would probably be amongst one of the first artifices used by a composer in any age; for, by this means, he would seek to prolong and continue an idea by repeating it upon a higher or a lower part of the scale than that in which he originally conceived it.* A Drone or *Pedal* Bass may also be counted as one of the earliest-used resources of polyphony; it being so easy to repeat or sustain one note at the same pitch, whilst another voice was made to sing a flowing melody against it by what, in after times, for the sake of distinction, came to be called *oblique motion.* Such an obvious and commonplace device—afterwards however, to be invested with so much poetic grandeur by the great composers before-mentioned, in the "Organ-points" of their Fugues, Oratorio Choruses, and other works—is to be found, perhaps, in its most rudimentary form in the first verse of "Jolly Rutterkin" (*see* the first bar after the refrain.)

A further and highly fruitful source of expression within the limited means of 15th Century composers lay in the constant change of rhythmical flow—from duple to triple sub-division of the semibreve pulsation, or *vice versa*—of which the Madrigals in this book afford so many interesting examples.

---

* *See,* for example, the first page of "I love, loved, and loved would I be," in which are two instances of Sequence.

A still more important element of composition was by no means unknown to musicians of this period, viz :—*Form* or *Design*. That very early formal design, the *Rondo*, is very clearly exemplified by two of the Madrigals, " Jolly Rutterkin " and " Margaret Meek," in which one principal theme constantly *comes round* again and again, by being recapitulated after the singing of certain episodical matter. Necessary relief and contrast are obtained by the intervening *episodes ;* whilst the repetition of the principal theme, which gets more and more familiar to the ear each time it is heard, is desirable in order that oneness of style and purpose may prevail instead of mere patchwork, or irrelevant ramblings. The more modern cyclical musical designs which depend entirely upon modulation, or change, balance, and proportion of key-relationships, we may not reasonably expect to meet with in these early compositions; yet we do find occasionally the recurrence of several figures of melody, and even the prevalence of certain harmonies standing to each other quite in the modern relation of tonic and dominant (*see* page 24), which are enough perhaps to show that the minds of 15th Century musicians were beginning in a slight degree to be influenced by the great *principles* of design which afterwards took more tangible shape, and to this day govern the feelings and ideas of composers.

As already pointed out, the harmonic results of music written in the Contrapuntal Epoch are but secondary. Every student knows that, as a rule, only triads and first inversions of the same are to be found in music of the " horizontal style." Still, these Madrigals furnish evidence of a reaching forward after a more highly developed style by the occasional use of harmonic combinations, which can only be regarded from a modern or fundamental view as so many direct or inverted Dominant Discords (*see* " The day day dawns "). Again, the dwelling upon certain mere chords (as in " I love, loved ") during the prevalence of which harmonies all melodic interest and separate part-individuality ceases, can only point to the anticipation of the " perpendicular style " in music. Such a yearning after harmonic effects for their own sake is continually to be detected in the Cathedral Music of those Early English Ecclesiastical writers who prepared the way for Henry Purcell, whose penetrating genius anticipated even those harmonic combinations which sound fresh to ears of to-day when met with in the most recent compositions of the musicians of the present time.

One of the greatest objections to music of the Contrapuntal Era—an objection

which would appear to be raised by modern musicians who do not exhibit much
sympathy with the feeling and manner of four or five centuries ago—may be said to
be occasioned by the constant appearance of what, at first sight, might be called
False Relation, viz: the inflection of a note by an accidental taking place in
a different part to that in which the note was first sounded in its normal pitch.
Frequent examples might be quoted from all the Church and Madrigal writers
of the Elizabethan period onwards as late as Dr. Croft, whose Anthem "We
will rejoice," furnishes as unpleasant a specimen as may be found in any work
of his predecessors for two centuries. *False Relation* at the present day is
defined as the awkward juxtaposition of distinct tonal-systems, caused by two
of the parts of successive chords proceeding in different keys at the same
instant, or nearly so. But as key-relationship (as we understand the term)
was unknown in the 15th Century, the many examples of what may at first
appear like *False Relation* in these Madrigals will require a little explanation.
It is this. We are here dealing with music written according to the
Ecclesiastical system of tonality in some one or other of the Church Modes,
where in certain cases an optional B flat (or B *molle* as it was called), was
allowed to be sung instead of the normal B natural or B *durum*. The
introduction of this optional note was merely for the sake of rendering the
particular part in which it occurred, smoother and easier to the singer as well
as more melodious to the listener. By its means the rugged interval of the
augmented 4th (or *tritone*) was dispelled, and various other inelegancies of
melodic progression were softened and improved, although sometimes—when
occurring in the midst of a sequence*—the *tritone* was not considered offensive
to the ear (*see* "I love, loved" treble part of last two bars in second score).
It mattered not if one part were singing B flat, and another part came in
with B natural on almost the next syllable, provided that the melodies of these
two parts were in themselves smooth and elegant. And since B natural and
B flat could both be said to belong to the same mode—one being *normal*, the
other *optional*—there could be no *False Relation*, at any rate in the modern
sense of the term. The primary and all-pervading provision for melodic
propriety, as something quite independent and apart from harmonic result,
makes itself felt in these Madrigals in many other ways, by the apparent

---

* *See* "Six Lectures on Harmony," by the late Sir G. A. Macfarren, Mus. Doc., M.A., formerly Professor
of Music in the University of Cambridge. Second Edition, pp. 58-9.

disregard of the ordinary first rules of Counterpoint ; notably those which forbid the progression of consecutive 5ths and 7ths and the use of discords by leap.* It does not follow, however, that 15th Century composers wrote with an utter defiance of rule, nor will it be consistent with history to regard their compositions as some sort of precedent for much that is wilful and lawless in music of the present day. It should be remembered that all Art-rules *follow* rather than precede Art-practice ; it being manifestly impossible to regulate anything which does not already exist. Hence many *experiments* in Part-writing had to be made before teachers and theorists could formulate rules for the guidance of students in Musical Composition. It is therefore in no spirit of captious fault-finding, that some of the more important deviations from rule have been here pointed out. These seeming irregularities may serve to illustrate the *experimental nature* of the Early Polyphonic School ; and it may also be both interesting and helpful to observe how far they are in accordance with the more successful breaches of established rule to be met with, not only in the works of modern composers, but in those of John Sebastian Bach and other classical writers.

Several of the Madrigals will be found somewhat difficult in performance on account of the unusual and unfamiliar rhythmical grouping of the notes. Evidently those who sang from the old unbarred single parts of the original MS., were in the habit of observing strict time in the most uncompromising manner possible, uninfluenced by what their fellow-singers might be doing, and marking the accents according to the natural rhythmical flow of the poetry. A stedfast and rigid counting of two or three in a bar is really all that is necessary for an accurate performance of the music as far as time is concerned.

In unbarred music, an accidental would necessarily affect only the note before which it was placed. This will account for the several additional accidentals of a contradictory nature, which become necessary when the music is barred. All accidentals which do not occur in the original MS. are, in this Edition, printed above the notes they are assumed to affect. A few

---

* *See*, for instance, the consecutive 5ths between the two lower parts in the last bar but two of *every* verse of "Margaret Meek," and also those in the second bar of the third verse of the same Madrigal. *See* also the consecutive 7ths between the two upper parts of the first two bars in the third score of "I love, loved," page 23. The two-part Madrigal "The farther I go" is also full of irregularities. Amongst many other instances, the use of a discord by leap in the second bar of the first score on page 22 deserves notice.

additional accidentals have been suggested here and there, with the view of affording occasional relief to the old modal tonality ; but these additions have, in all cases, been placed *over* the notation, so that they may not be taken as part of the original. Such suggestions can, however, be either wholly or partially accepted, or, they may be entirely disregarded, according as taste or feeling may prompt.

These accidentals have been added in accordance with the rules of Musica ficta (lit. *false* or *feigned music*), which was a term used to express certain notes which, it is assumed, were chromatically raised or lowered a semitone in actual performance, but which were not accidentally sharpened or flattened in the notation of the written parts. These alterations, said to have been made by singers, and intended and sanctioned (though not *indicated*) by composers, may have come into use for the two reasons of harmonic propriety, and of melodic smoothness. Without these additional but unwritten inflections (i.) certain dissonant harmonic combinations (or *chords* as we should now call them) would have been called into existence, which the system of timing then in vogue would have rendered more or less offensive to the ear ; and (ii.) many passages of melody would have presented here and there rough edges and sharp corners, ungrateful alike to both singer and listener. It is, of course, very doubtful whether these accidentals, as added in this volume, are actually required or not ; many musicians of the present day who are skilled in reading old music think that there was no fixed practice for their use.* Our ears have grown so accustomed to modern tonality, that it is exceedingly difficult for us to realize the old tonal feeling which possessed those who sang and wrote four centuries since. With this difficulty before us, the following quotations from Mediæval theorists, extracted from a Paper entitled " The Flat, Sharp, and Natural," by Mr. Frederick Niecks, which was published in the *Proceedings of the Musical Association, Sixteenth Session*, 1889-90, may prove interesting if not helpful.

JOHANNES DE GARLANDIA, who probably wrote in the second half of the 12th Century, is already quite on the modern standpoint in dividing all tones into semitones. He says : " *Falsa musica* (which is very necessary for

---

* *See* remarks by Mr. T. L. Southgate on page 98 of "Proceedings of the Musical Association, Sixteenth Session, 1889-90."

instruments, especially for the organ) arises when we take a semitone instead of a tone, or the reverse.   Every tone is divisible into two semitones, therefore the number of the signs which indicate the semitone may be increased in all the modes."[*]

FRANCO OF COLOGNE at the end of the 12th Century writes : " When the *discantor* cannot get useful consonances by right music (*recta musica*) he may at his pleasure make false music (*musica falsa*)."

WALTER ODINGTON, who wrote somewhat later, in the first half of the 13th Century, does not go quite so far as Johannes de Garlandia, but he adds to B♭, which formed part of the regular system, the notes F sharp, C sharp, and E flat, saying "the double B [B♮, B♭] effects, according to the moderns, a double F [F♯, F♮] and a double E [E♮, E♭]; and the double F effects a double C [C♯, C♮], in order that for both, perfect fifths may be found."

He explains also how the raising and lowering of a note is indicated respectively by a square ♭ and a round ♮, and adds : "The two B's belong to the monochord ; the other alterations are called by musicians *falsa musica* not because they contain anything dissonant, but because they are outside the disposition of the monochord, and were not used by the ancients."[†]

JOHANNES DE MURIS, a writer of the 14th Century, says that "the false mutations (*mutationes falsæ*, viz., the chromatic alterations other than B♭) are contrary to the character of plain-song, but that it is otherwise with mensurable song " (by which we have to understand ' harmonic music ').

PROSDOCIMUS DE BELDOMANDIS, who wrote at the beginning of the 15th Century, says that "the chromatic semitones of *musica ficta* were used for no other reason than to produce a more pleasing harmony."

In an Italian MS. of the 14th Century occur the words " False music ought not to be indicated (*Non debet falsa musica signari*), and the Italian Pietro Aron says in "Il Toscanello in Musica" (the first edition of which appeared in 1523), "Accidentals are not needed by learned and practical singers, but are

---

[*] *Introductio Musicæ Secundum Magistrum Garlandia* in Vol. I., p. 166, of Coussemaker's "Scriptores de musica medii ævi.   It is worthy of notice that in the Madrigal "Jolly Rutterkin" (page 1, score 1, bar 2) the use of B♭ and B♮ occurs in the same bar.   This is an interesting instance of a fifteenth Century composer disregarding the strict limits of the diatonic modal tonality.

[†] *Fratris Walteri Odingtoni De Speculatione Musicæ*, in Vol. I., page 215, of Coussemaker's "Scriptores."

inserted only for inexperienced and unintelligent ones." Both Zarlino and
Zacconi, in the latter half of the 16th Century, write much to the same effect.

DR. CARL PROSKE, the editor of "Musica Divina" gives the following rules
for supplying the necessary accidentals of *Musica ficta* :—

(i.) The perfect cadence at the end of a piece, and those occasionally to
be found in the course of it, must have one part proceeding to the
final by a semitone (or, as we should say, the leading note going to
the tonic).   The last chord of a perfect cadence must end with a
major third (or, as we should say—in dealing with a modern minor
key—the " Tierce de Picardie " should be made use of).

(ii.) To avoid the false relation of the tritone (*mi contra fa*), the augmented
fourth and diminished fifth have to be modified wherever they occur.

(iii.) When (as in our scale of C) the note B is preceded by A, and descends
immediately afterwards, this B is to be flattened, especially if it returns
to A.   The same thing takes place in the scale of F, with one flat in
the signature where E is flattened in similar circumstances.

(iv.) In two parts a minor sixth proceeding to the octave (each part moving
a second) is often changed into a major sixth.

CHRISTOPHER SIMPSON, on page 40 of the 1678 edition of his "Compendium
of Practical Musick," distinctly states that, except in the perfect cadence, the
use of the accidentally raised seventh of the minor mode "is disputable, as
many times it happens in musick ; in which doubts the Ear is always to be
Umpire."

An *instrumental* bass part has been added to the two-part Madrigal "The
farther I go," in the style and tonality of the voice parts.   This is intended
for the violoncello.   One or more instruments should be used according to
the number of voices employed ; in no case should the voice parts themselves
be duplicated instrumentally.   It is possible that this may originally have been
a three-part Madrigal, of which the under voice-part has been lost.   No
additional accidentals have been suggested for the voice parts of this Madrigal ;
but it will be quite easy to add a few according to the rules of *musica ficta*
given above, if any such inflections should be thought desirable in performance
when the voices are *unaccompanied* by the added instrumental bass part.

In the place of an ordinary accompaniment, a compressed pianoforte score
has been added, which represents faithfully the vocal parts so far as the relative

time value of their notes is concerned ; but which is written entirely in modern notation, *i.e.*, in notes of such time value as will render the proper rate of movement of the music perfectly intelligible to the uninitiated musical reader. With this object, the minim has been adopted as the average unit beat note in place of the semibreve of the original notation.   This method of printing the compressed score is in accordance with a similar plan pursued by the editors of " Dutch, Latin, French and Italian Masters of the XV. and XVI. Centuries," Berlin, M. Bahn, 1873.

My best thanks are due to my friend and master Dr. E. J. Hopkins, organist of the Temple Church, and Vice-President of the Society, for many valuable suggestions in connection both with the foregoing remarks and with the preparation of the music for the press.

C. W. P.

II.—THE NOTATION.

For the purpose of enabling readers to verify the translations into barred music of the examples in *facsimile*, a few remarks are necessary.

In modern notation every note equals two of the next lower denomination, but musicians of the 13th Century had formulated the rule that the normal note contained three of those of next less value, so that the *Long* contained three *Breves*, and the *Breve* three *Semibreves*. The converse of the lengthening power of the *dot* had therefore to be effected, and · the triple value of the note was reduced to duple by grouping it with a smaller one, so that the two together were equal to the full value of the perfect note. Hence Triple time came to be called *Perfect*, and Duple time *Imperfect*, when in the 15th Century time signatures came into use, and the former was expressed by the circle, the symbol of perfection, and the latter by the semicircle. Before the invention of the Italian indications of *tempo*, musicians were also obliged to adopt an absolute time value for each note, so that in order to show that a composition was to be taken in quick time, a line was drawn through the time signature to signify that the notes were of half their normal length. In the modern versions now given this distinction is expressed in the usual way, and not by using notes of half value.

The rules of the 13th Century composers for time measurement were of extreme complexity, especially for the *Ligatures, i.e.*, note-groups either in the form of rhomboids or of notes joined by strokes, but by the date of the present specimens they had become much simplified. The Imperfect time signature reduced the notation almost to our present system, but when in Perfect time, the notation followed the old rule of a breve containing three semibreves, except when reduced a third by grouping with a semibreve.

The forms of the notes, except for being angular, are the same as the modern, with the exception of the Long, which is a Breve with a tail, and of the rhomboidal Ligatures. The notes indicated by these rhomboids are those of the lines or spaces on which the figure begins and ends ; the intervening ones are of no account whatever.

The greater notes were either written full or hollow, according to the taste of the scribe, but if written full, the crotchet (being of the same shape as the minim), and the quaver and semiquaver were in red. If the greater notes were written hollow, then the lesser ones were in black, as in our modern notation, and as in the facsimiles given, some of which in the original MS. (Add 5465), were in full (black) and red. But breves, semibreves, and minims, were also written in red or full (black) to indicate: 1°, that the phrase was in triplets if they occurred in a duple measure, and either with or without a small 3 before the phrase; 2°, that they were in duple time if occurring in a triple measure, and 3°, that they were of only half the time-value of the rest of the composition. All these varieties of the use of the red or full notes occur in "*This day day dawns*," where slight differences in *tempo* are shown by the varying use of 1° and 3°.

Rests followed the rules of the notes, and the student will perceive that here also, if in perfect time, a following small note reduced the value of the rest by a third.

Longs, breves, and semibreves, were also united in Ligatures, in survival of the earlier forms of notation, and to indicate sometimes that two or more notes were sung to one syllable. The notes might be either square, joined by position or by a tail, or in rhomboidal form as explained above.

The rules for the interpretation of Ligatures are as follows, the value of the notes varying according to the time signature (*vide* Pl. A). It must be remembered that in Perfect time a note was diminished one-third by a following note of the next lower value.

The First Note.

1°. If without a tail and higher than the next, it is a *Long* (*a*).

2°. If without a tail and lower than the next, it is a *Breve* (*b*).

3°. If it have a downward tail on the right, it is a *Long* (*c*).

4°. If it have a downward tail on the left, and be either higher or lower than the next, it is a *Breve* (*d*).

5°. If it have an upward tail on the left, then it and the following note are both *Semibreves* (*e*). This rule, therefore, governs final and intermediate notes, except when in very rare instances it conflicts with rules 9 and 10, when only the first note is a *Semibreve*.

THE LAST NOTE.

6°. If square and lower than the preceding note, it is a *Long* (*f*).

7°. If rhomboidal and either higher or lower, it is a *Breve* (*g*).

8°. If without a tail and higher than the preceding note, it is a *Breve* (*h*).

9°. If with a downward tail on the right, it is a *Long* (*i*).

10°. If with an upward tail on the right it is a *Breve*.

THE INTERMEDIATE NOTES are all Breves (*k*), except when they have downward tails on the right, when they are Longs, or, when with an upward tail on the left they come under Rule 5 (*l*).

All notes may have their value increased one-half by a dot.

A stroke joining two notes is not accounted a tail. If one note stand directly above the other it is the lower that is first sounded.

The ordinary time signatures, providing for the sub-division of the Breve, are as on Plate A. It will be observed that a dot inserted in the circle or semicircle makes the semibreve contain three minims. The minim and lesser notes always contain two of the next lower value.

The sub-division of the Long was provided for by prefixing to the time signature a stroke, or two uneven strokes, drawn through three spaces, to signify that the Long contained three Breves—*Lesser Mode perfect.* Without any stroke or with two even ones through two spaces, the Long contained two Breves—*Lesser Mode imperfect.*

In like manner, three strokes through three spaces, divided the *Maxima*, or Double Long, into three Longs—*Greater Mode perfect*, and two *even* strokes through three spaces, signified its normal double value—*Greater Mode imperfect.*

The Greater and Lesser Modes were prefixed to any of the time signatures which indicated the sub-division of the Breve.

It will be of assistance to students to call attention to a few peculiarities in the Madrigals besides those mistakes in the MSS. which are noted on the Plates. These errors, which are all connected with *Rests*, are so plainly due to the scribe, that they were probably detected by the singer without any trouble.

"*Jolly Rutterkin.*"—This is in *perfect* time and it will accordingly be noticed that the *Long* rest at the beginning of the first alto part, verse IV., is equal to two breves each containing three semibreves.

"*Margaret Meek.*"—The time signature is entirely omitted in the MS.

"*This day day dawns.*"—By an error of the scribe the time signature of only the treble part has the line through it signifying that the notes are to be taken double their normal pace. At A the time changes to perfect, and from there to B the notes are of half their previous value, because written full. The rests at C, which remain in imperfect time, prove this peculiarity, while the following full notes are also of half value and in perfect time, though preceded by no time signature. On the other hand, the full notes at D preceded by a 3 are of their full value, except in so far that they are triplets against rests at G, in imperfect time. The exigencies of modern notation require that the bar completing the triplet phrase ending E should be considered in connection with the first note of the phrase. An apparent readjustment of the rests at F also becomes necessary, but it will be found that the time is strictly preserved throughout.

"*The farther I go.*"—The final note-form in all the parts is translated as a single note. In all the Madrigals great diversity occurs in the form of the final note, which differs often in the several parts and verses. It would appear, therefore, as if it were held *ad libitum*.

"*I love, loved, and loved would I be.*"—The treble throughout and the bass of the verses are written, as in the *facsimile*, without a flat signature, but there can be little doubt that the flat was intended to apply to all the parts.

"*I love, I love, and whom love ye.*"—Only the first treble and alto have the signature for *Imperfect time with prolation*, which might be translated as $\frac{6}{8}$, but the second treble has equivalent notes in triplets, as will be seen on the repetition of the phrase at A, which also proves the inaccuracy of the scribe in the omission and insertion of rests. The different verses of this Madrigal in the original show many slight discrepancies. The time signature is in red and therefore apparently applies only to the full notes, as the first hollow minim is certainly in imperfect time *without* prolation.

H. B. B.

III.—THE MANUSCRIPTS.

No. 58 of the Appendix to the Royal MSS. in the British Museum, contains the voice parts (most of them apparently of solos for a tenor voice), and a few instrumental parts and scores for the virginals and lute, of an interesting collection of pieces by some little-known musicians of the beginning of the 16th Century. The MS. cannot have been written before 1503, if the song "Now fayre fayrest off euery fayre" alludes, as is supposed, to the marriage of Margaret, sister of Henry VII., with James IV. of Scotland, which took place in that year. A note on f. 1 in an early, almost contemporary, hand connects the volume with the diocese of Exeter.

Among the principal compositions are :—an instrumental piece in three parts by John Ambrose ; "Petyously constrayned am I," by Dr. Coper ; "Now marcy Jhesu I wyll amend" ; Frere Gastkyn wo thow be" (treble part only), by Raff Drake ; "Egredientem de templo" ; part of a Mass beginning "Et in terra pax" and ending with the "Agnus Dei" ; a Hornpipe in score, by Hugh Astone ; "My Lady Careys dompe" ; "My Lady Wynkfylds rownde" ; "The Emperorse pavyn" ; "The Kyngs pavyn" ; "The Kyngs Maske" ; "The Whele of Fortune" (with the words) ; "The Duke of Somersetts dompe" in lute notation ; "Thys endere nyzth I saw a syzth," with chorus ; "My lytelle fole is gon to play," in three parts ; *etc.*

(*Small obl. Quarto. 58 folios.*)

Additional MS. 5465 contains an equally interesting collection of part-songs, most of them for three voices, with a few for two and for four voices, by composers of the end of the 15th Century. The volume is supposed to have belonged to Robert Fairfax, the composer, whose arms are inserted in the initial letters of one of his compositions (p. 26 *b.*) ; it certainly belonged to Charles Fairfax in 1618, after which it passed into the hands of Ralph Thoresby of Leeds, the Antiquarian. Among the most considerable pieces are :—"What causyth me wofull thoughtis," for two voices, by William Newark ; "Yowre counturfetyng," the bass part of which is marked "ad placitum" ; "Sumwhat musyng," by Roberd Fayrfax ; "I loue I loue and whom loue ye," by Syr Thomas Phelyppis ; "A my dere son sayd Mary" ; "Jhesu mercy how may this be," for four voices, by Browne ; "Affraid alas and whi so sodenli"; "Woffully a raid my blode man for the ran," by William Cornyssh, junior; "A gentill Jhesu," for four voices, by Sheryngam; "Woffully a rayd," for four voices, by Browne; "My feerful dreme," by Gilbert Banastir; "A blessid Jhesu," by Richard Davy; "Margaret Meke," by Browne; "Ay be sherewe yow," by William Cornyssh, junior; "Hoyda hoyda joly rutterkyn," by the same; "From stormy wyndis," by Edmund Turges; *etc.* *

Most of the pieces are headed with ornamental initial letters, in blue and red.　　　*(Quarto,* 124 *folios.)*

Additional MS. 31,922, consists of a collection of part-songs, mostly for three voices, and instrumental pieces, by Henry VIII. and other English composers, who lived not later than the early part of his reign. From internal evidence the collection must have been compiled after 1511, and the present copy was perhaps made at the end of the king's reign. Among the vocal pieces are:—" Pastyme with good companye," " Helas madam cel que jeme tant," " Grene growith the holy," by the king; " Blow thi horne hunter," " Thow and I and Amyas," by Cornish; " Quid petis o fili," in two parts, by Pygott; " Englond be glad, pluk up thy lusty hart," " My thought oppressed," " Sumwhat musyng," " Hey troly loly lo mayde whether go you," by anonymous composers. The principal instrumental pieces are a " Fa la sol," extending over ten pages, by an anonymous composer; two three-part compositions by Flude, elsewhere called J. Fluyd [*al.* Lloyd?], described as " in Armonia graduat," to the tenor of one of which pieces is appended the words " Iste tenor ascendit a gradu epadoico (sic) in semitonium et descendit in diatessaron cum diatonico"; a three-part piece by Dunstable, with the following explanatory lines (!), added to the four notes of which the quasi-ground tenor appears to consist :—" A dorio (sic) tenor sic ascendens esse videtur, quater per genera tetracordum refitetur"; and a three-part composition by Fayrfax, at the end of which is written " Paremese tenor—Canon. Pausa facta

---

* " *I love, I love, and whom love ye*" and " *This day day dawns* " have evidently a political meaning. The former may have been put forth as a feeler to test public opinion in the year 1460, when the Duke of York was about to claim the throne in place of the imbecile Henry VI. From the careful suppression of the name of the flower it may be placed in the first half of the year, before the Yorkist party had come into power by the Battle of Northampton.

The latter song is the complement of the other, and probably appeared early in 1461, when Edward IV. was proclaimed King in London, though perhaps the allusion to the flower-de-luce might indicate the year 1471, when the King of France was helping the Lancastrian party.

J. T. M.

in tenore de numero perfecto secundum prohemium percantetur omnis litera arsum (Sic) et thesum per naturam sinaphe."

This volume appears to have belonged in the 16th century to several families in the parish of Benenden, Kent; among later owners are Thomas Fuller, *M.D.*, Archibald, 11th Earl of Eglinton, and Sir Charles Montolieu Lamb. It is in the original binding of wooden boards, covered with stamped leather. (*Small Folio.* 129 *folios*).

ORIGINAL TEXT OF THE SONGS.

To leve alone comfort ys none
But mornyng more and more
My awne tru hart hath made me smart
Whyche grevyth me passyng sore.

I may complayne and nothyng fayne
To God of my lady
Wythoute grete unryght out of hur syght
She hath exylyde me.

Hur to dysplease my lyf to lease
Never shall tyll I dye
How be hyt in payne I am sertayne
And beryth hyt paciently.

And so I wyll contynew styll
Wherever I ryde or goo
I cannot chewse nor yet refewse
To love hur and no mo.

One and no mo why say ye soo?
O thus ys the skyl . . . . .
Few yerys agoo I promysyd soo
For to be tru h . . . . .

Kytt hathe lost hur key hur key
Goode Kytt hath lost hur key
She ys soo sory for the cause
She wottes not what to say.

Kytt she wept I axyde why soo
That she made all thys mone
She sayde alas I am soo woo
My key ys lost and gone.

Kyt she wept and cryede one hye
And fore hur key dyd axe
She be heyght to seynt sythe a key
And offryde to hym a key of wexe.

Kyt why dyd ye losse your key?
Fore sothe ye were to blame
Now ev'y man to yow wyll say
Kyt lossekey ys youre name.

Kyt she wept and cryed alas,
Hur key she cowde not fynde
In faythe I trow yn bour' she was
W't sum that were not kende.

Now farewell Kytt I can no more
I wot not what to say
But I shall p'y to Gode therefore
That you may fynde yo' key.

A the syghes that come fro my hert
They greve me passyng sore
Syth I must fro my love depart
Farewell my Joye fore evermore.

Oft to me wyth hur goodly face
She was wont to cast an eye
And now absence to me in place
Alas! for woo I dye I dye.

I was wonte hur to beholde
And takyn in armes twayne
And now wyth syghes manyfolde
Farewell my Joye and welcome payne.

A ! mythynke that I se hur yett
As wolde to Gode that I myght
There myght no joyes compare wyth hyt
Unto my hart to make hyt lyght.

———

THOUGH that she can not redresse
Nor helpe me off my smerte
Yet sure hyt comyth of gentylnesse
That pytyeth a mornynge hert.

O fortune cruell and pervers
What aylyth the at me
All my plesure thow dost revers
Into Adversite.

Alas I love a goodly one
But I cannot attayne
Unto hur love but lyve alone
For fere of fals dysdayne

To have hur love I thenke me sure
Yf that she durst consent
Hyt ys to hur a displesure
To se my love mysspentt.

O Cupyd the god of love
Now helpe me at my nede
The hartes of them for to remove
That lettyth me to spede.

Woo worth fortune my sortall foo
That art soo rude to me
To turne my joy in care and woo
That my comfort sholde be.

IN May that lusty sesoun to geder
The flours downe by the medows grene
The byrdys sang on euery syde so meryly
It ioyed my hart they toyned so dene
The nyghtyngale sang on hie ioyfully
So merely among the thornys kene.

———

THE lytyll prety nyghtyngale
Among the leuys grene
I wolde I were wyth hur all nyght
But yet ye wote not whome I mene.

The nyghtynggale sat one a brere
Among the thornys sherpe and keyne
And comfort me wyth mery chere
But yet ye wot not home I mene.

She dyd apere all on hur keynde
A lady ryght well be seyng
With wordys of loff tolde me hur mynde
But yet ye wot not whome I mene.

Hyt dyd me goode apone hur to loke
Hur corse was closyd all in grene
Away fro me hur hert she toke
But yet ye wot not whome I mene.

Lady I cryed wyth rufull mone
Have mynd of me that true hath bene
For I loue none but you alone
But yet ye wot not whome I mene.

INDEX TO THE THREE MSS.

A. H.—H.

SONGS.

———

Kitt hath lost her kye.

Accompt by C. W. P.

Voice

Allegretto quasi Siciliano.

Pianoforte

Kitt hath lost her kye, her kye, Good Kitt hath lost her kye, She

is so sor - ry for the cause She knows not what to say, She is so

sor - ry for the cause She knows not what to say, to say, Good Kitt Good

(a) The original minim is not dotted

Kitt she is so sor..ry for the cause She knows not what to

say, to say,. Good Kitt

Fine.   *meno mosso*

1. Kitt she wept, I asked why _ so That
2. Kitt why did you lose your kye? For
3. Kitt she wept, and cried a _ las! Her

Fine.   *meno mosso*

Fine.   *il Basso legato*

she made all this moan ; She said "A _ las! I
sooth you were to blame; Now eve _ ry man to
kye she could not find ; In faith I trow in

staccato

(a)   (a)   (a) *Da Capo al Segno.*

am so woe My kye is lost and gone".
you will say "Kitt Lose _ kye" is your name.
byre she was With some that were not kenn'd.

Da Capo al Segno.

(a) These notes are crotchets in the original

Alone I live.

Melody by Dr Cooper.
Accomp! by C. W. P.

A _ lone _____ I live, a _ lone;

And sore __ I sigh for _____ one A _ lone _____

_____ I live a _ lone; _____ And sore I sigh _ for one __

sigh _____ for one

_p_

A _ lone I live a _

_pp_

Da Capo al Segno.

_ lone; And sore I sigh _____ for _____ one

Da Capo al Segno.

To live alone.

Melody by John Cole.
Accompt by C. W. P.

Voice

Andantino

Pianoforte

p legato

To
But

1. To live a _ lone com _ fort _____ is none _____
2. I may com_plain and no _____ thing fain _____
3. But so I will con _ ti _____ nue still _____

legato il basso

live a - lone ____ comfort is ____ none
may complain and so ____ thing fain
so I will con . ti ____ nue still

But mourning more ____ and more ____
To God of my ____ la . dy ____
Wher . e'er i ride ____ or go ____

con passione

My own true heart ____ hath made me smart ____
With great un . right ____ out of her sight ____
I can . not choose ____ nor yet re . fuse ____

My
With
I

own true heart hath made me smart
great un . right out of her sight
can . not choose nor yet re . fuse

Which grie . veth me ____ passing sore ____
She hath ex . il ____ ed me ____
To love her and ____ no ____ more

which grie . veth me passing sore ____ *after last verse*

____ *after last verse*

(a) No minim rest in original

In May, that lusty season.

Melody by Thomas Farthing.
Accompt by C. W. P.

Voice

Pianoforte

Allegretto.

In May that lus - ty sea - son to ga - ther the

flo - wers in the meadows green

the flowers in the mea - dows green

The

dim. - in - u - en - do

(a) This minim rest is not in the original

birds sang on every side so mer_ri_ly _____ it joy'd my heart _____ they tu_ned so _____ clean _____ The night _ in _ _gale sang _____ on high joy_ful_ly so mer_ri_ly _____ among the thorns _____ keen _____ In

Da Capo al Segno.

(b to c) Original version

The nightingale.

Accomp! by C. W. P.

Original Key a fifth lower

Voice

Allegro con spirito

Pianoforte.

di _ mi _ nu _ en _ do

1. The   lit _ tle   pret _ ty
2. She   did   ap _ pear   all
3. La _ dy   I   cried with

cresc.   *dim.*

nigh _ tin _ gale   A _ mong   the leaves so   fair _____ and
of   her   kind   A   la _ dy   fair right well _____ be _
rue _ ful   moan   Have   mind   of   me   that true _____ hath

mf

green _____   I   would I   were   with her   all   night _____
seen _____   With   words of   love   told   me   her   mind _____
been _____   For   I   love   none   but   you   a _ lone _____

ral _ _ len _ _ tan _ _ do

But yet ye know__ not whom__ I mean

ral _ _ len _ _ tan _ _ do

Though that she cannot redress.

Accomp! by C. W. P.

Voice

Pianoforte.

Larghetto espressivo

pp

1. Though that she can _ not re _ dress Nor help me of my smart __
2. To have her love I think me sure If that she durst con _ sent __
3. Ah woe to fate my mor _ tal foe That art so rude to me __

Yet sure it comes of gen _ tle _ ness That pi _ ti _ eth a bro _ ken heart
It is to her a dis _ plea _ sure To see my faith _ ful love mis _ spent
Turning my joy to care and woe That tru _ est com _ fort now should be

after last verse.

* This note for verses 2 and 3 only.
(a)(b) These notes are semibreves in the original.

Ah! the sighs.

Accomp! by C. W. P.

Voice

1. Ah! the
2. Oft to
3. Ah! me_

Andantino

Pianoforte.

p   cresc.   p

sighs that   come from my   heart ____   They   grieve   me   pas_sing   sore ____
me   with   her good_ly   face ____   She   used   to   cast   an   eye ____
think that   I   see her   yet ____   As   would   to   God   I   might ____

Since   I   must   from   my   love   de ____ part ____
But   ab_sent now   from   eve _ ry ____ place ____
Then   would   no   joys com _ pare with ____ it ____

ral _ _ _ len _ tan _ do

Fare _ well   my   joy   for ever   more. ____
A _ las   for   woe I   die, I   die! ____
Un _ to   my   heart to make it   light. ____

colla voce

MADRIGALS.

Jolly Rutterkin.

W. Cornish jr.

*) The Time - Signature indicates ⁷⁄ or three semibreves, the semibreve being the unit or beat - note. The Compressed Score is in ³⁄ or modern three - minim time, the minim being the beat - note.

This Refrain is to be sung after each verse **I**

Fine

In a

Rutterkin is come un.to our town   In a

Rutterkin is come un. to our town   In a

This Refrain is to be sung after each verse **I**

Fine

Repeat Refrain on page 1

cloak without coat or gown

To ____ cover his crown like a rut . ter

cloak without coat or gown save a rag.ged hood to cover his crown   Like a rutter

cloak without coat or gown save a rag.ged hood to cover his crown like a rutterkin

Repeat Refrain on page 1

II

Rut.terkin can speak no Eng . . lish   His   tongue runneth all on buttered

Rut.terkin can speak no Eng . . lish

His tongue runneth all on buttered fish

II

Repeat Refrain on page 1

fish Be-smeared with grease a-bout his dish Like a rut - ter

Be-smeared with grease a-bout his dish Like a rutter

Be-smeared with grease a-bout his dish Like a rut - ter

Repeat Refrain on page 1

III

A stoup of beer up at a pluck

Rut-terkin shall bring you all good luck A stoup of beer up at a pluck

Rut-terkin shall bring you all good luck A stoup of beer up at a pluck

III

Till his brain be as wise as a duck

Till his

Till his brain be as wise as a duck

Repeat Refrain on page 1
IV
Like a rut - ter.
brain be as wise
as a duck
Like a rutter.
Ere Rutter-kin from
Like a rut - ter.
Ere Rutter-kin from
Repeat Refrain on page 1
IV
He will drink a gal-lon
pot full at twice
board will rise
He will drink a gal-lon
pot full at twice
And the o - verplus
board will rise
He will drink a gal-lon
pot full at twice
And the o - verplus
Repeat Refrain on page 1
And the o - verplus
that's on the ta - ble of the new
guise Like a rut - ter
of the new
guise
Like a rut. ter
that's on the ta - ble of the new
guise
Like a rut - ter
Repeat Refrain on page 1

Margaret meek

Browne

so pret_ti_ly she deals al ways
_ways so pret_ti_ly she deals always
so pret_ti_ly she deals always she
she deals al ways
she deals always
deals al_ways
II
That goodly lass when she me has a_
That goodly lass when she me has a_las, a_las, a_
a_las, a_las
II

_las a_las I wot not where I go — or stand
las I wot not where I go or stand
a_las I wot not where I go or stand
I think me bound on sea on land to comfort her
I think me bound on sea on land to comfort her
on sea on land to com_fort her to
to comfort her
to comfort her to comfort her
com_fort her to comfort her

so manner - ly
so manner - ly
so man - ner - ly
so
so
courteously
so
pret - ti - ly
she deals always
so
courteously
so
pretti - ly
courteously
so
pretti - ly
she
deals
she deals al - ways
al - ways
so pret - ti - ly
she deals
so
so
pret - ti - ly she deals al - ways

al ways she deals al
pret-ti-ly she deals al-ways she deals always
she deals al-ways
ways
III
Her lusty cheer her yes most
Her lusty cheer her yes most
III
I know no peer in her beau ty both Kate and
clear I know no peer in her beau ty both Kate and Bess Maud and A-
clear in her beau ty both Kate and Bess

Bess Maud and Avice   Cis is witness   Cis is wit.ness   Cis is wit — ness

...vice   Cis is witness   Cis is wit.ness   Cis is wit.ness

Maud and Avice   Cis is witness   Cis is wit.ness _____

of her fealty _____   of her feal.ty _____

of her fealty _____   of her feal.ty

of her fealty _____   so man.nerly _____

so manner.ly   so courteously so pret.ti.ly _____

so man.nerly _____   so courteously so

so courteously so pretti.ly _____

she deals always
pretti - ly
she deals al - ways
she deals al - ways
so
so pret - ti - ly she deals al ways she
so pret - ti - ly she deals al - ways
pret - ti - ly she deals al - ways she deals al - ways
IV
deals al ways
My Marga - ret I can
she deals always
My Marga - ret I can
My Marga - ret I can
IV

_not meet _ _ _ in field or street wo_

_ful am I _ wo_ful am I _

not meet _ _ in field or street

wo_ful am I

_not meet _ in field or street woful am

I _ _ wo_ful am I _

_but leave this chance _ your cheer ad_vance _

but leave this chance _ your cheer _ ad_

but leave this chance _ your cheer ad_vance your cheer_ ad_

and let us dance
hark my la - dy hark my la -
-vance and let us dance
hark my la - dy
hark my la -
-vance
hark my la - dy hark my la - dy
dy
hark my la
dy
dy hark my la
dy
hark my la - - dy
hark my la - dy
hark my la - dy
so manner-
so manner-ly
so courteously so
so
so man-nerly
so
ly
so courteous-ly so preti-ti - ly

pret - ti - ly
she deals always
courteous_ly so
pret_ti_ly
she deals al - ways
she deals al - ways
so pret - ti - ly she deals
al
ways
so
pret - ti_ly she
deals al_ways
so
pret_ti_ly she deals al_ways
she
she
deals al
ways
she
deals always
deals al_ways

This day day dawns

gentle day dawns
And we must home go

gentle day dawns this gentle day dawns And we must home go *) and

this gentle day dawns And we must home go

and we must home go and we must home go

we must home go we must home go

we must home go we must home go we must home

This refrain is to be sung after each verse

Fine

we must home go

Fine

In a glo — ri — ous gar — den
In that gar — den be flow — ers

go In a glo — rious gar — den
In that gar — den be flowers

This refrain is to be sung after each verse

Fine

*) The words in italics are not in the original

saw I sit - ting a come - ly queen
the gelo - sir gent that she well knew
green
of hue
saw I sit - ting a come - ly
the gelo - - sir gent that she
green
of hue
saw I sit - ting a come - ly
the gelo - sir gent that she well
A - mong the flowers that fresh bin a mong the
The flower de luce she did un - rue the flower de
queen
well knew
A - mong the flowers that fresh bin
The flower de luce she did un - rue
queen
knew
A - mong the
The flowers de
flowers that fresh bin she gathered a rose and set be -
luce she did un - rue and said the white rose is most
she gathered a rose and set be -
and said the white rose is most
flowers that fresh bin she gathered a rose and set
luce she did un - rue and said the white rose is most true

-tween
true
The
This
-tween The li - ly white rose me thought I saw
true This garden to rule by right eous law
be - tween the li - ly white rose me thought I saw
this gar - den to rule by right - eous law
li - ly white rose me thought I saw and e - ver she
gar.den to rule by right - eous law
The li - ly white rose me thought I saw and e - ver she sang
This gar.den to rule by right - eous law
The li - ly white rose me thought I saw and e - ver
This garden to rule by right - eous law
Repeat refrain
sang this day day dawns this day day dawns this gen - tle day day dawns
this day day this day day dawns This gen - tle day dawns
she sang this day day dawns This gen - tle day dawns
Repeat refrain

The farther I go.

William Newark.

Treble The far - ther I go the more be - hind _____

Alto The far - ther I go the more be - hind _____

Voice Parts

*)**Added Bass**
Part by C. W. P.

the more be - - hind

the

the _____ near - er _____ my ways _____

more be - hind the _____ near _____ er _____

*) For Violoncello.

end
my ways end
the
the more I seek the worse can I
more I seek the worse can I
find
find
the light - er
the light - er
love the lo - wer for to wend
love the lo - wer for to wend

The tru-er I serve

The truer I serve

the farther out of mind

the far - - ther out

though I go loose

of mind though I go loose

yet am I tied with a line

yet am I tied with a line

It is fortune or un_for_tune this I

It is fortune or un_for_tune this

find

I find

I love, loved, and loved would I be.

Robert Fairfax.

Then bound - en were I
Then bound
Then bound - en were I
such one faithful - ly to love Though I do fear
- en were I such one faithfully to love Though I do fear
such one faithful - ly to love Though I
to trace that dance
to trace that dance
do fear to trace that dance

Lest ___ that mis ad - ven -

Lest ___ that mis ad - ven -

Lest ___ that mis ad - ven -

_ture might fall by chance yet will I me trust to

_ture might fall by chance ___ yet will I me trust to

_ture might fall by chance ___ yet ___ will I me trust to ___

1

for _ tune ap _ ply   How that ev _ _ er it will hap   I know   not

for _ tune ap _ ply How that   ev _ er it will   hap   I   know   not I _

for _ tune ap _ ply How that   ev _ er it   will   hap   I   know   not

I love, I love, and whom love ye?

Refrain

Sir Thomas Phillips.

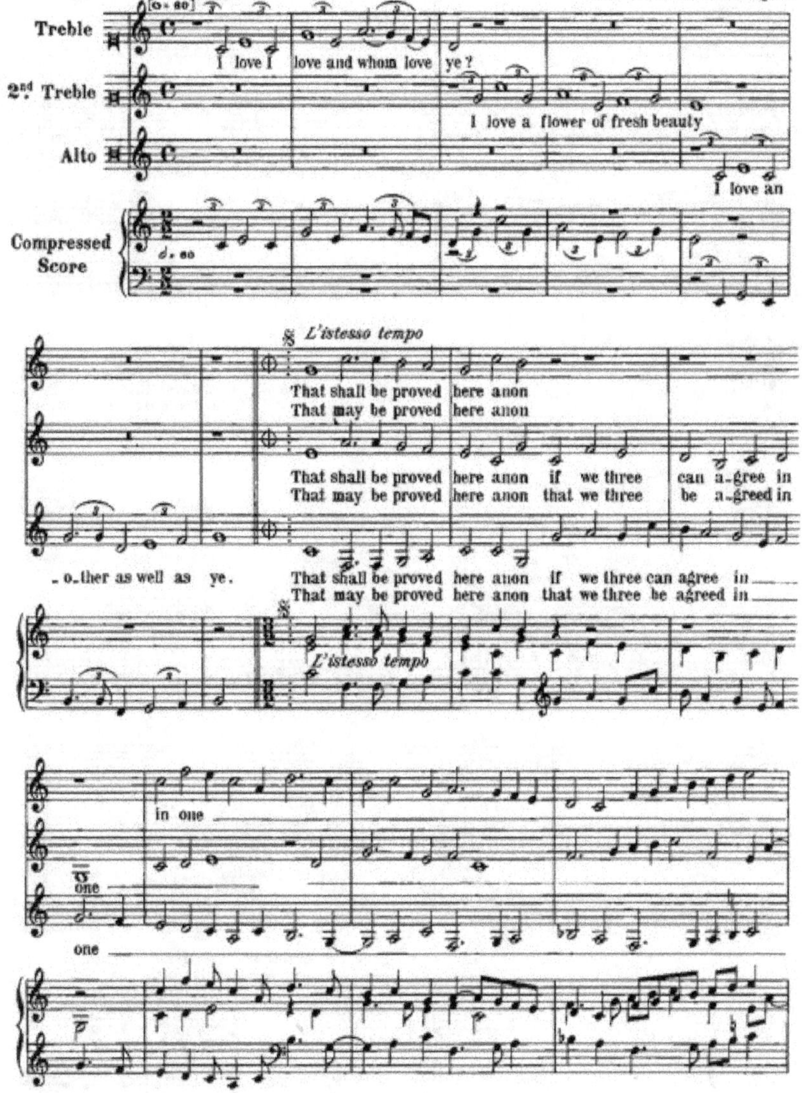

I love a flower of sweet o ____ dour
There is a flower wher - e'er he ____ be

mar - jo
which shall

I love a flower of sweet o dour mar -
There is a flower wher - e'er he be which ____

Col _ umbine gold _ en of sweet fla vour
Prim _ rose vi _ o _ let or fresh dai _ sy

_ram gen _ tle or la _ ven ____ der
not yet be named for ____ me

_ jo _ ram gen _ tle or la ____ ven _ der Col _ umbine gold _ en of sweet fla ____ vour
_shall not yet be na _ med for me Prim _ rose vi _ o _ let or fresh dai ____ sy

nay
h'es

let be 'tis none of them that li _ keth me
past them all in his de _ gree that best li _ keth

nay
he's past

let ____ be 'tis
them ____ all in

none of them that ____ li _ keth me
his de _ gree that best li _ keth me

let be 'tis none of them that li _ keth me ____
them all in his de _ gree that best li _ keth me ____

I love I love and whom love ye? I love a flower of fresh beau-
I love a flower of fresh beau-
I love I love and whom love ye? I love
Da Capo al Segno
III and IV
ty
The rose it is a roy-al flower
I love the rose both red and white
ty I love an-o-ther as well as ye
The red
Is that
I love an-o-ther as well as ye
The rose it is a roy-al flower the
I love the rose both red and white is
Da Capo al Segno
both be full sweet and of like sa-vour
to hear talk of them is my de-light
or the white shows his co-lour
your pure perfect ap-pe-tite
red or the white shows his co-lour both be full sweet and of like sa-vour
that your pure per-fect ap-pe-tite to hear talk of them is my de-light

all one they be that day to see it li-
joy ed may we be our Prince to see and ro-
all one they be that day to see it li-keth
joy ed may we be our Prince to see and ro-
they be that day to see it li-keth well
we be our Prince to see and ro-ses three
keth well me now have I lov'd and whom love ye I love a
ses three now have we lov'd and love will we this fair fresh
well me I love a
ses three this fair fresh
me now have I lov'd and whom love ye I love
now have we lov'd and love will we this flower
Da capo al segno
flow'r of fresh beau-ty
flow'r full of beau-ty
flow'r of fresh beau-ty I love an-o-ther as well as ye
flow'r full of beau-ty most wor-thy it is as think-eth me
I love an-o-ther as well as ye
most wor-thy it is as think-eth me

If love now reigned.

By King Henry VIII.

Values of notes in the Ligatures

Note. In the above the tied Breves are to be considered as the equivalent of a Long 𝕼 in the Lesser Mode imperfect

Perfect time
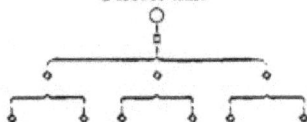

Perfect time with prolation
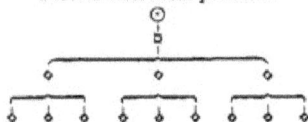

Imperfect time
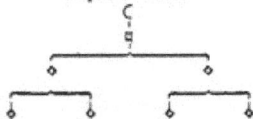

Imperfect time with prolation
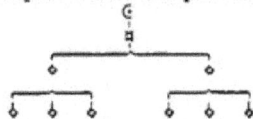

Lesser Mode perfect
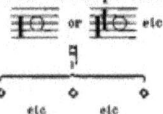

Lesser Mode imperfect
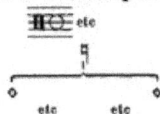

Greater Mode perfect
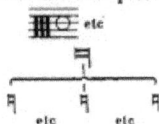

Greater Mode imperfect
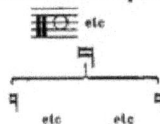

Jolly Rutterkin.

Wm. Cornish Jr

(a) This note should apparently be hollow.   (b) The flat must be a mistake and intended for the B.

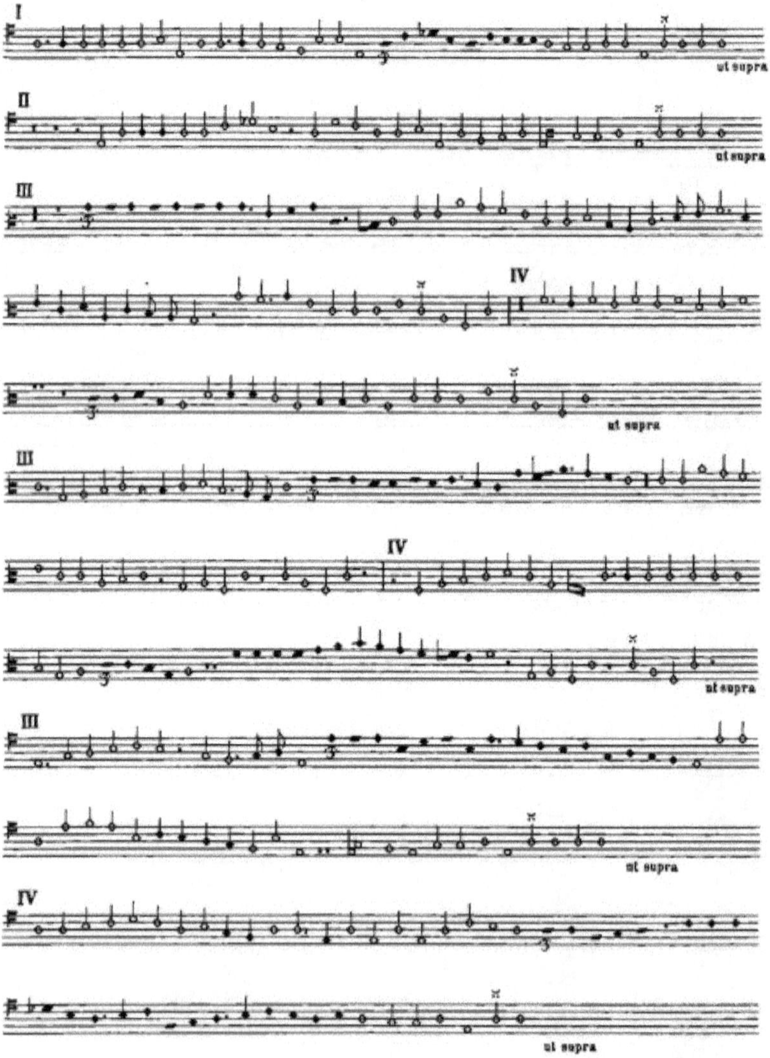
I
ut supra
II
ut supra
III
IV
ut supra
III
IV
ut supra
III
ut supra
IV
ut supra

This day day dawns.

Anon

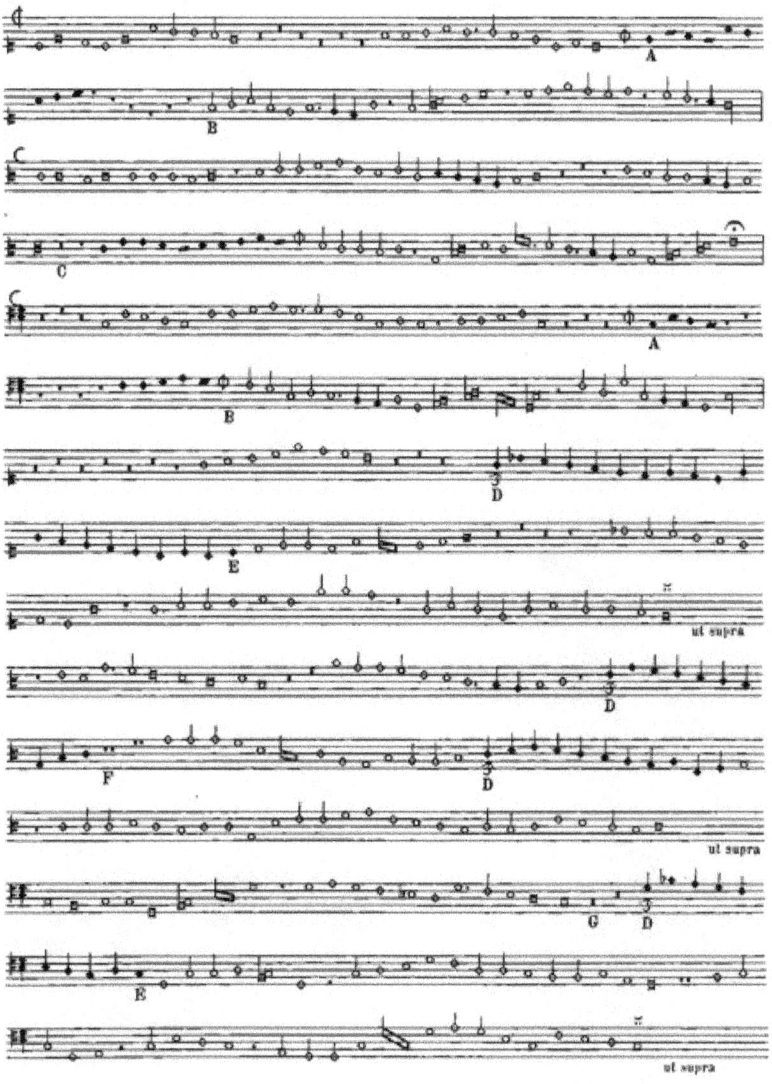

The farther I go

William Newark

I love, loved, and loved would I be.

Robert Fairfax

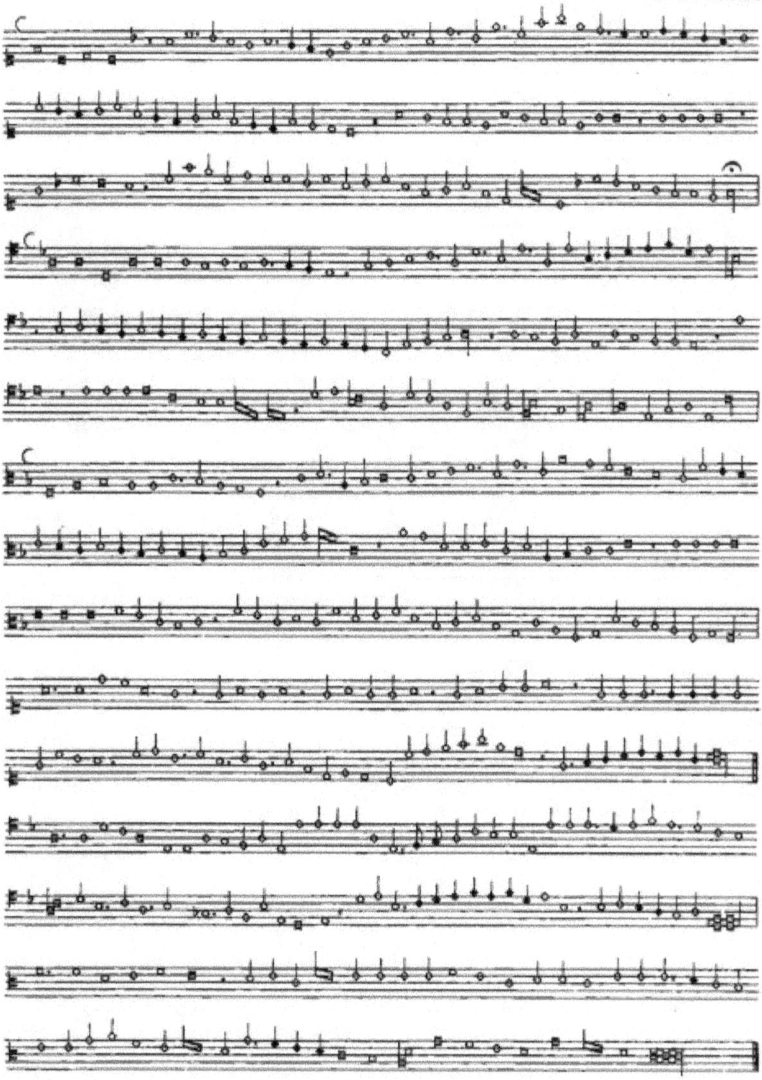

I love, I love and whom love ye?

Sir Thomas Phillips

(a) two semibreve rests are apparently omitted in the *m. s.*

Margaret meek.

Browne

ut supra

ut supra

ut supra

ut supra

ut supra

(a) no rest should be here

ut supra

IV

ut supra

IV

ut supra

IV

ut supra

(a) This should be a semibreve rest.